3011205074907 3

GW01281006

Books for young people

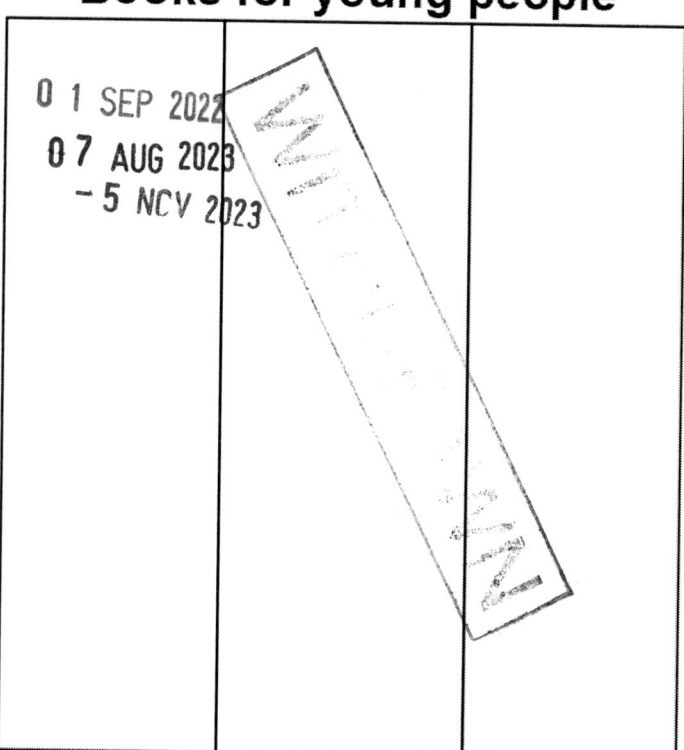

0 1 SEP 2022
0 7 AUG 2023
- 5 NOV 2023

Please look after this book and return it on time
Books issued to an adult card will incur fines for late returns.
Renew on our website below,
by phone or in person.

HILLINGDON
LONDON

www.hillingdon.gov.uk/renew

LIFE CYCLE OF A SALMON

By Kirsty Holmes

LIFE CYCLES

Words that look like **this** can be found in the glossary on page 24.

BookLife PUBLISHING

©2021
BookLife Publishing Ltd.
King's Lynn
Norfolk PE30 4LS

ISBN: 978-1-83927-478-7

All rights reserved. Printed in Malta.

All facts, statistics, web addresses and URLs in this book were verified as valid and accurate at time of writing. No responsibility for any changes to external websites or references can be accepted by either the author or publisher.

Written by:
Kirsty Holmes

Edited by:
Emilie Dufresne

Designed by:
Gareth Liddington

A catalogue record for this book is available from the British Library.

PHOTO CREDITS

Front Cover – azure1, schankz, 2 – EB Adventure Photography, 4&5 – epsco studio, Gratsias Adhi Hermawan, Kang Sunghee, Dean Drobot, eungchopan, Ruslan Huzau, Odua Images, 6&7 – Alexander Raths, Shannon Heryet, 8&9 – KhunYing, Ronnie Chua, Kevin Cass, 10&11 – OpenCage, U.S. Fish and Wildlife Service Northeast Region, 12&13 – jack perks, U.S. Fish and Wildlife Service Northeast Region, 14&15 – Tory Kallman, Aristokrates, 16&17 – Chanonry, Krasowit, Beat J Korner, 18&19 – Zureks, Gleb Tarro, Kirsanov Valeriy Vladimirovich, Nina B, 20&21 – Chanonry, Heidi Besen, 22&23 – BMJ, Zykov_Vladimir, Peter Steenstra, Jakub Rutkiewicz. Images are courtesy of Shutterstock.com. With thanks to Getty Images, Thinkstock Photo and iStockphoto.

LIFE CYCLE OF A SALMON

Page 4	**What Is a Life Cycle?**
Page 6	**Super Salmon**
Page 8	**Excellent Eggs**
Page 10	**Amazing Alevins**
Page 11	**Fantastic Fry**
Page 12	**Smart Smolts**
Page 14	**Smashing Salmon**
Page 16	**Life as a Salmon**
Page 18	**Fun Facts about Salmon**
Page 20	**The End of Life as a Salmon**
Page 22	**The Life Cycle**
Page 24	**Glossary and Index**

WHAT IS A LIFE CYCLE?

Baby

Toddler

Child

All living things have a life cycle. They are all born, they all grow bigger, and their bodies change.

Teenager

Adult

Elderly Person

When they are fully grown, they have **offspring** of their own. In the end, all living things die. This is the life cycle.

5

SUPER SALMON

Salmon are animals. They are **fish**. They have long bodies and different fins, including a tail fin. They have scales on their skin, and gills to breathe through.

Fins

Scales

A fish uses its gills to breathe in water.

Tail Fin

Gills

The salmon makes an incredible journey.

Atlantic salmon live in the ocean as adults and travel back to the fresh water where they were born to make babies of their own. They remember where to go using their **senses**.

EXCELLENT EGGS

Can you see the tiny black dots inside the eggs? They are the eyes of the developing **salmon**.

The mother salmon lays her eggs in the riverbed. The eggs are small, about the size of a pea, and they are bright orange.

The mother will dig a small nest in the gravel on the riverbed. This is called a redd. She will lay her eggs here.

The mother covers her eggs with more gravel to protect them.

AMAZING ALEVINS

When the baby salmon hatch they are called alevins. They keep the **yolk** from their eggs attached to their bodies.

The alevins use the yolk for food.

Alevin

Yolk Sac

FANTASTIC FRY

Parr Marks

Parrs have markings known as parr marks. These help to camouflage them.

Once the yolk sac has been used up, the alevins become fry. They are now big enough to come out of the gravel and look for food. They carry on growing until they become parr.

SMASHING SALMON

Atlantic salmon enter the sea as smolts and live their adult life there. Adults have silvery skin.

A grilse is a salmon that has been at sea for one winter before returning to the river it came from.

Salmon eat small fish and shrimp. They spend their time at sea eating and growing, until they are ready to travel back to the fresh water they came from and make more salmon.

LIFE AS A SALMON

Salmon Jumping
Upstream

When the salmon are ready to lay their eggs, they will swim back to the river they came from. The salmon often have to leap and jump to get upstream.

When they reach the river, the females dig their redds and lay their eggs. The males **fertilise** the eggs on the riverbed, and the life cycle begins again.

FUN FACTS ABOUT SALMON

- The largest type of salmon is a chinook salmon. They can grow to over a metre long!

- Bears like to eat salmon as they return to the rivers. They catch them as they leap!

- Adult male salmon often have a hooked jaw, called a kype.

Kype

- Salmon can travel hundreds or even thousands of miles to get back to the river they hatched in.

THE END OF LIFE AS A SALMON

Humans also like to catch and eat salmon.

Salmon have to look out for many **predators**, both in the sea and in the river. Bears, sharks, dolphins, seals and sea lions all eat salmon.

When the salmon have finished laying and fertilising the eggs, most of them run out of energy and die. Scientists think they get old very quickly at the end of their life.

When the salmon have laid or fertilised eggs, they are called kelts.

THE LIFE CYCLE

A salmon's life cycle has different stages. Each stage looks very different from the last.

Egg

Alevin

Parr

The eggs hatch and the alevins grow and gain parr marks. The smolts head out to sea. The adult salmon swim back to the river to lay their eggs.

Smolt

In the end, the salmon dies and the life cycle is complete.

Adult

GLOSSARY

camouflage parts that allow an animal to hide itself
developing growing and changing
fertilise to make an egg grow into a new animal
fish an animal that has gills and lives in water
offspring the young of an animal or plant
predators animals that hunt other animals for food
sac a part of a plant or animal that is shaped like a pouch
senses the things that allow animals to be aware of the world around them, such as smell and sight
upstream against the way the water flows in a river or stream
yolk the part of an egg which gives food to the animal growing inside it

INDEX

alevins 10–11, 22–23
eggs 8–10, 16–17, 21–23
fry 11–12
kelts 21
oceans 7, 13
parrs 11, 13, 22–23
redds 9, 17
rivers 8–9, 13, 15–20, 23